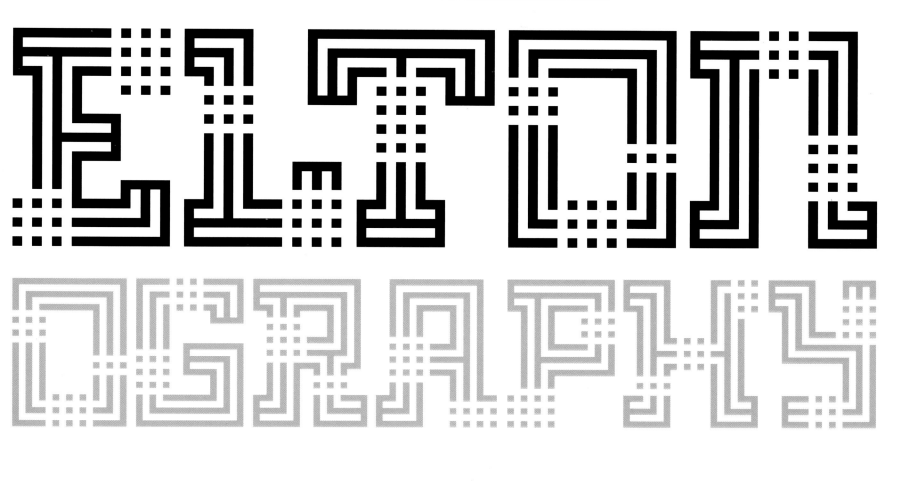

TERRY O'NEILL'S

ELTON
OGRAPHY

A LIFE IN PICTURES
SIR ELTON JOHN
BY TERRY O'NEILL

PUBLISHERS EVANS MITCHELL BOOKS

The Old Forge, 16 Church Street, Rickmansworth, Herts WD3 1DH, United Kingdom. Email info@senateconsulting.co.uk

© Evans Mitchell Books. Printed 2008. **WWW.EMBOOKS.CO.UK**

Contents

MOST OF THE PHOTOGRAPHS IN **ELTONOGRAPHY** HAVE NEVER BEEN PUBLISHED. TERRY O'NEILL'S RELATIONSHIP WITH SIR ELTON JOHN SPANS FOUR DECADES AND CHART, IN PUBLIC AND IN PRIVATE, **ONE OF THE GREATEST STORIES IN THE ROCK 'N ROLL HALL OF FAME.**

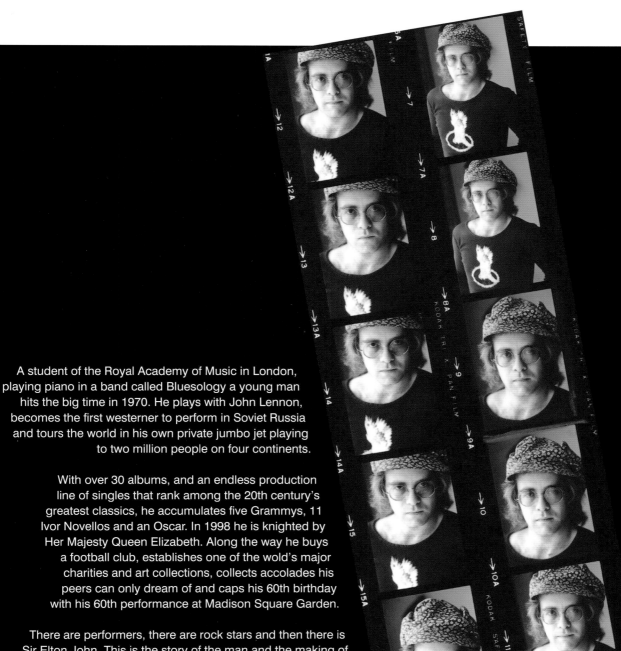

A student of the Royal Academy of Music in London, playing piano in a band called Bluesology a young man hits the big time in 1970. He plays with John Lennon, becomes the first westerner to perform in Soviet Russia and tours the world in his own private jumbo jet playing to two million people on four continents.

With over 30 albums, and an endless production line of singles that rank among the 20th century's greatest classics, he accumulates five Grammys, 11 Ivor Novellos and an Oscar. In 1998 he is knighted by Her Majesty Queen Elizabeth. Along the way he buys a football club, establishes one of the wold's major charities and art collections, collects accolades his peers can only dream of and caps his 60th birthday with his 60th performance at Madison Square Garden.

There are performers, there are rock stars and then there is Sir Elton John. This is the story of the man and the making of the legend – his life, in pictures, from his earliest adventures on the trail of fame to the hallowed halls of superstardom. Intimate, exhausting, passionate, private, Elton at work, Elton at play, Elton on the road, Elton at home, Elton the clown, Elton the rock star, Elton the man behind the myth.

Terry O'Neill's camera has chronicled the careers of the greatest names in showbusiness, from Frank Sinatra and The Beatles to Hollywood stars. But no-one appeared before his lens more than **Sir Elton John**. What began as a photo-shoot with the new kid on the pop block in the early 70s, developed into a friendship and photographic partnership that spanned decades. This book is the legacy of that relationship. It is called the **Eltonography** because it is an exhaustive biography of the landscape of a mesmerising life; a stunning collection of photographs many never seen before, drawn from an archive of thousands that will trigger memories, amazement and surprise at the breadth of Sir Elton John's Life In Pictures.

Left: The first photo shoot: Just plain Elton John in 1972

It's not just the music, **it's the man**, not just the life but the legend.

MORE THAN 250 MILLION ALBUMS SOLD, 100 MILLION SINGLES, AN OSCAR, FIVE GRAMMIES, AND PERHAPS THE MOST SUCCESSFUL, SUSTAINED, SUPERLATIVE, ROLLERCOASTER JOURNEY IN THE HISTORY OF ROCK 'N ROLL – AND PHOTOGRAPHER TERRY O'NEILL WAS RIDING SHOTGUN.

UP THERE WITH ELVIS, THE BEATLES, THE STONES, AND THE IMMORTALS IN THE PANTHEON OF POP, SIR ELTON JOHN PIONEERED ROCK PIANO, ALMOST SINGLE-HANDED INVENTED THE BIG STADIUM CONCERTS AND WAS THE FIRST WESTERN STAR TO PART THE IRON CURTAIN AND PERFORM IN THE OLD SOVIET UNION.

IN 1972 WHEN THIS PORTRAIT WAS TAKEN (LEFT) THE YOUNG ELTON JOHN, ALREADY AN ACCOMPLISHED MUSICIAN, COMPOSER AND VOCALIST WAS ABOUT TO BREAKTHROUGH WITH HIS FIRST NO 1 ALBUM, HONKY CHATEAU, WHICH SPAWNED THE SINGLE ROCKET MAN.

IT WAS A PROPHETIC AND APTLY NAMED HIT. LEGALLY CHANGING HIS NAME FROM REGINALD KENNETH DWIGHT, THE CAREER OF ONE OF THE PLANET'S MOST FLAMBOYANT MEN WAS LAUNCHED...

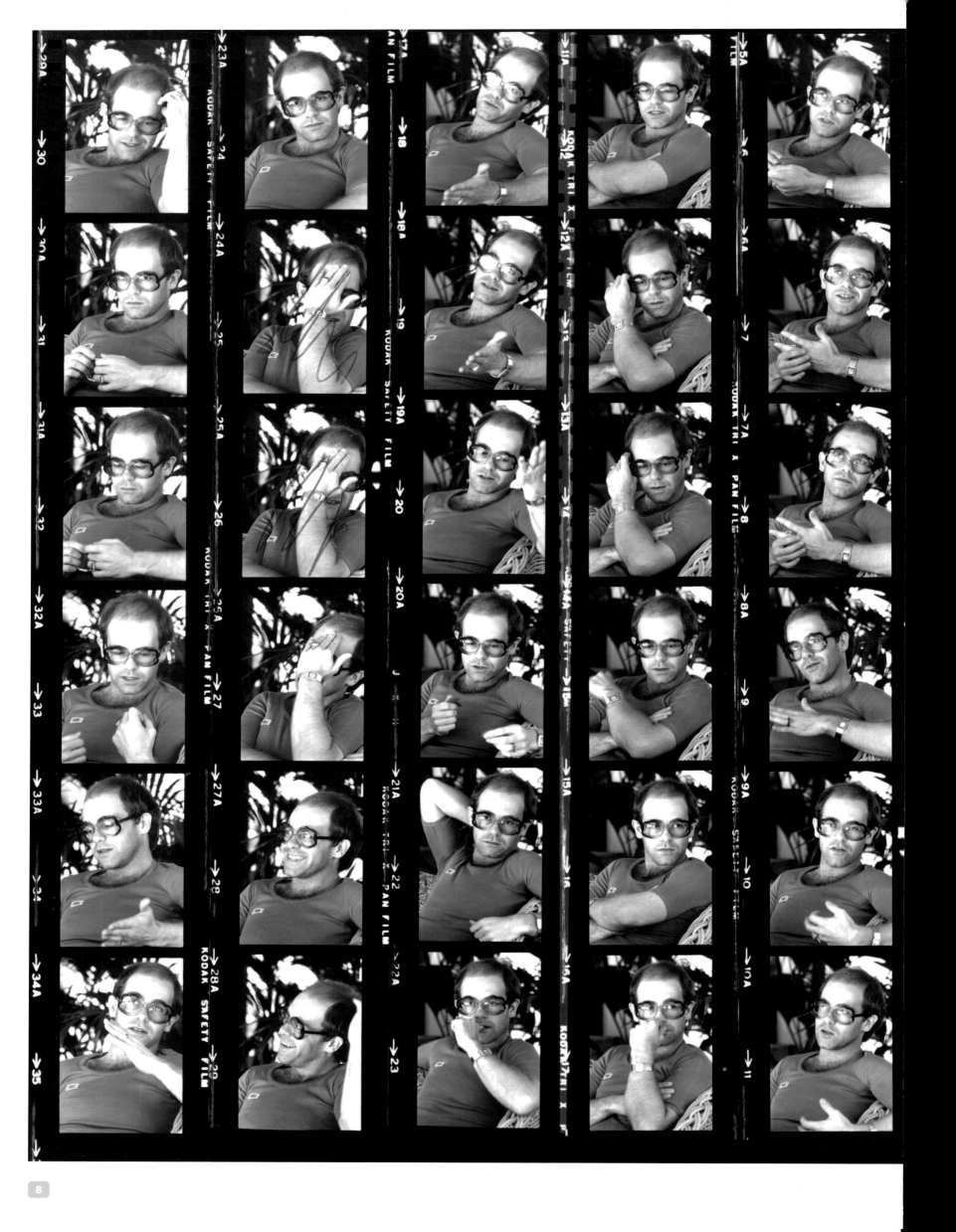

1972: The story begins. Terry O'Neill's first photo-shoot with the emerging rock star

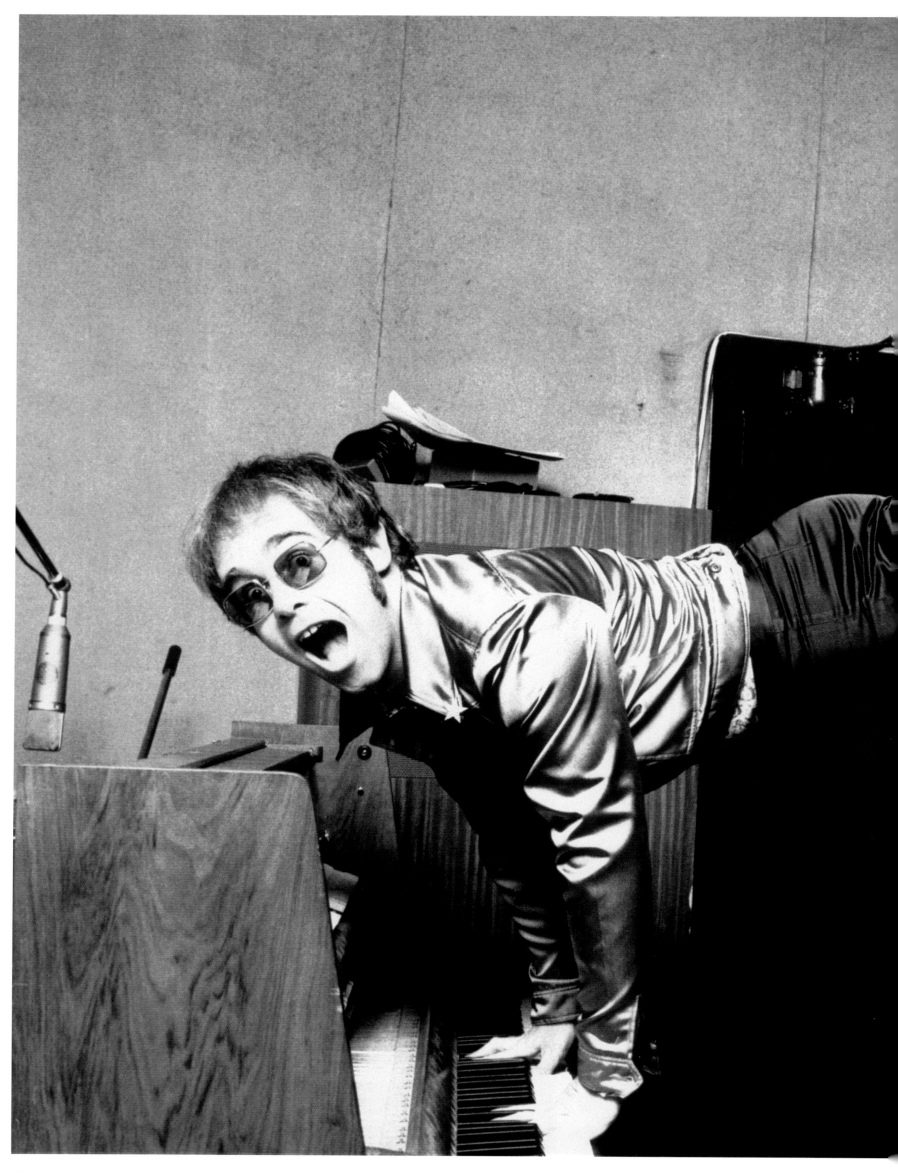

Keyboard hand stands were already a hallmark of Elton's stage act performance and a hint of the high-octane, energised concerts to come

The success of *Honky Chateau* made Elton a household name – alongside Sir Michel Caine, seen here in an early recording of Britain's most successful chatshow with host Michael Parkinson

By 1974 the trappings of fame and success had purchased a luxurious home outside London and a passion for costume that was to be a hallmark of his career

Early on in his career Elton John recognised that to fill a stadium with 100,000 fans, a star needed to be seen as well as heard – and that meant clothes that were part of the performance

Go on, shoot me.
I'm the piano player

IN 1972 HE WAS PLAIN REGINALD KENNETH DWIGHT PREPARING TO CHANGE HIS NAME AND RELEASE HIS FIRST SMASH HIT ALBUM **HONKY CHATEAU.** BY 1975 HE HAD A GLOBAL HOUSEHOLD NAME, FIVE MORE HUGE HIT ALBUMS WITH 50 MILLION SALES, EIGHT PLATINUM DISCS AND EIGHT NO 1 SPOTS IN US/UK CHARTS.

ELTON JOHN WORKED FURIOUSLY BOTH IN THE STUDIO AND ON TOUR. HE HAD BECOME THE HOTTEST ROCK ACT ON THE PLANET AND IN THOSE ACCESSIBLE, EXCITING DAYS OF THE EARLY 70s, STARS WEREN'T AFRAID TO SHOW THEIR PRIVATE FACES IN PUBLIC. STALKERS AND THE SLAYING OF JOHN LENNON HAD YET TO FORCE CELEBRITY INSIDE "LOCK DOWN" SECURITY CORDONS AND ELTON WELCOMED **TERRY O'NEILL** INTO HIS HOME FOR THIS CANDID RECORD OF HIS EARLY DAYS...

Always the performer, from the moment he got out of bed in the morning

A day in the life of a rock star starts with the newspapers, half a grapefruit and a gulp of apple juice at the kitchen table

26

The bookshelves in his library said it all – music, soccer, art and fashion with a few modern classics but surprisingly little verse for a man famed for the poetry of his music

Elton with a rare 1975 10-inch bootleg album of John Lennon, which bears the famous advice of Lennon's Aunt Mimi *A guitar's all right John but you'll never earn a living by it*

The record and tape collection filled a room at Elton's house – now he can carry it all on an iPod

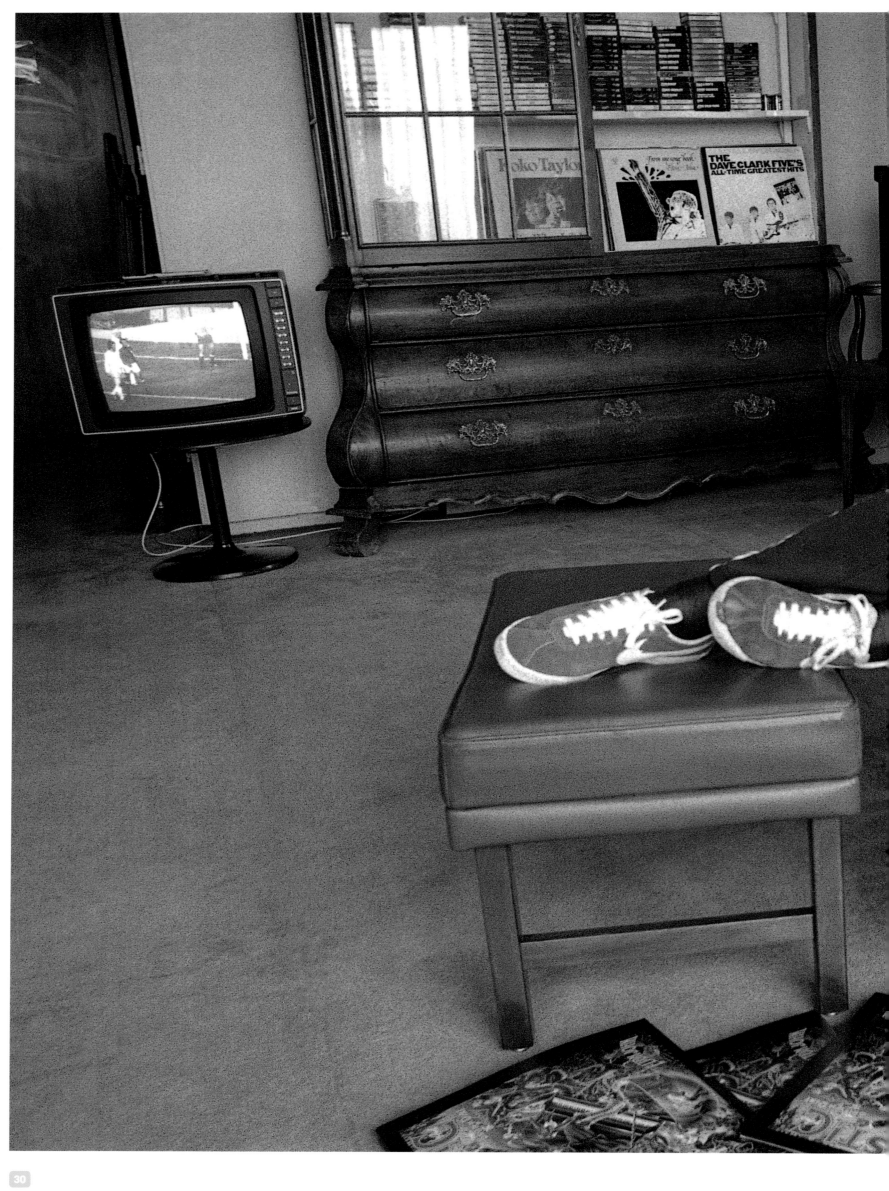

A soccer game on the TV, and a pile of albums to sign. Captain Fantastic would sell 7 million copies and reach No 1 in the US charts (UK No 2) – his fifth No 1 album in under three years

Elton John's mother Sheila encouraged him to perform in pubs and clubs from the age of 15...

but it was his grandmother Ivy who started him out on the piano when he was just four years old

Early Elton: the process of acquiring one memorable publicity shot involved multiple locations, changes of clothing and moods

The bags are packed – he's ready to go. In the 70s Elton was always on the go, averaging up to three albums a year and countless concerts

Among his pride and joy was an enormous collection of rare and vintage motorcars

Shooting the images for the 1978 hit album *A Single Man*, O'Neill posed Elton in a rare, vintage fixed-head, Jaguar XK

Fasten your seatbelts: The year Elton John took the world by storm

Elton arrives in Los Angeles aboard his private jet decked out for his 1975 tour and containing all the comforts of home.

On board, in bed: at 30,000ft between cities on the hectic 1975 concert schedule

The Boeing jetliner came equipped with a bar, and piano with a no smoking sign that the band clearly didn't see

In the garden of his rented house in Beverly Hills

Elton is fitted with his famous butterfly suit – and a photo opportunity with a mountain of fan mail

In October 1975 **Elton John** performed two sell out concerts...

TO FANS IN LOS ANGELES' DODGERS'
STADIUM – IT WAS A MUSICAL
EXTRAVAGANZA ROCK FANS HAD NEVER
SEEN THE LIKE OF, AND PRODUCED
PERHAPS THE MOST IMMORTAL
IMAGES OF **ELTON** IN THE
TERRY O'NEILL ARCHIVES

Among the fans: Cary Grant, Elton's close friend, tennis champion Billie Jean King and British broadcaster Russell Harty

Backstage with Billie Jean King (above) while two costumed security men play a practical joke on the boss

Rehearsals seemed to be never-ending...

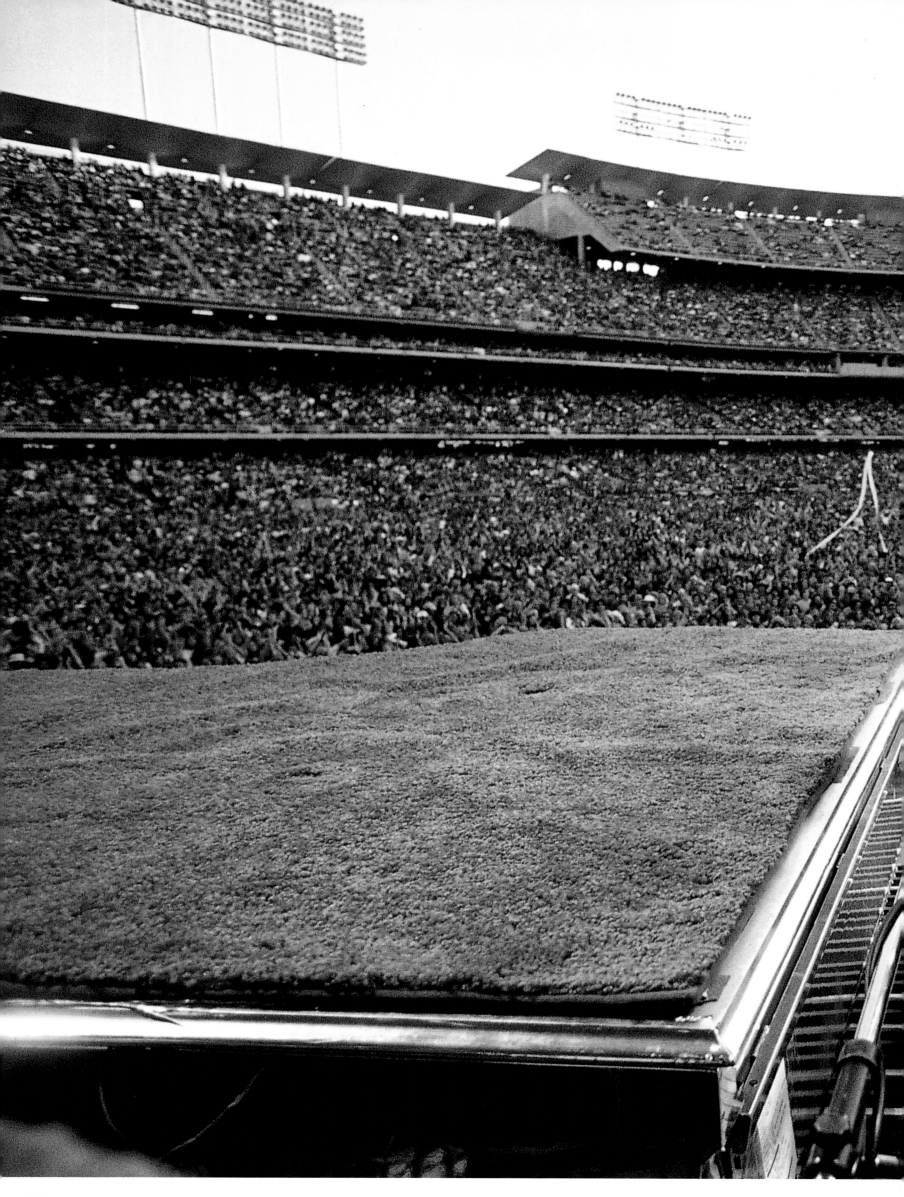

The show begins: Elton's appearance in a sequined Dodgers' baseball kit had the crowd on their feet before he sang a note

More than 100,000 people packed the stadium over two days – Elton John was the biggest box office act in the world

Elton had released his *Rock Of The Westies* album just prior to the concert – his second album that year after *Captain Fantastic*

Always the showman: Elton's concerts were no just about music, but entertainment. His empathy with a concert crowd was second to none

During a break in rehearsals, Elton, the band and Terry O'Neill (bottom left rubbing his jaw) enjoy an impromptu kickabout

"AFTER TWO DAYS IN THAT
STADIUM HE WAS WIPED OUT.
I DON'T THINK I'VE EVER
SEEN ANYONE WORK SO HARD
IN MY LIFE, BE SO DEDICATED
TO PUTTING ON A SHOW
THAT THE CROWD WOULD
REMEMBER FOR THE
REST OF THEIR LIVES.

IT'S BEEN OVER 30 YEARS
SINCE THE DODGERS'
BUT YOU JUST DON'T
FORGET AN EVENT LIKE THAT.
IT WAS A ONCE IN A LIFETIME
THING"
TERRY O'NEILL

The other love of his life

In 1976 Elton bought a lowly small town soccer club, Watford FC and installed a youthful unknown coach with innovative ideas, called Graham Taylor

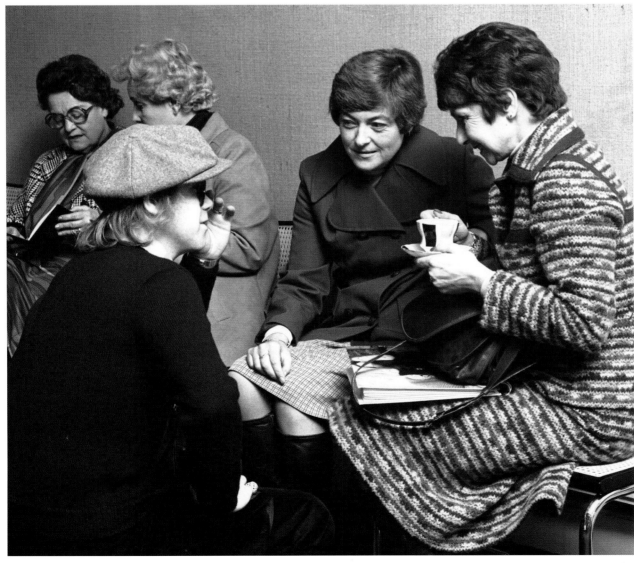

Elton set about transforming Watford into a family friendly club with mother and children enclosures that would pioneer a new era in English soccer

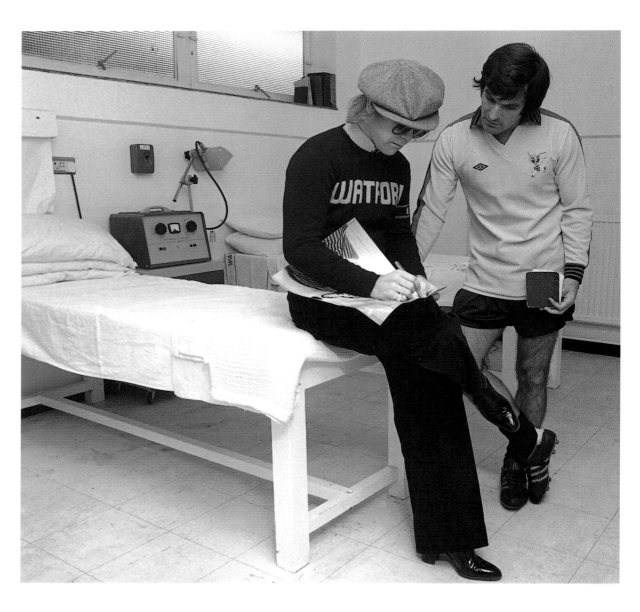

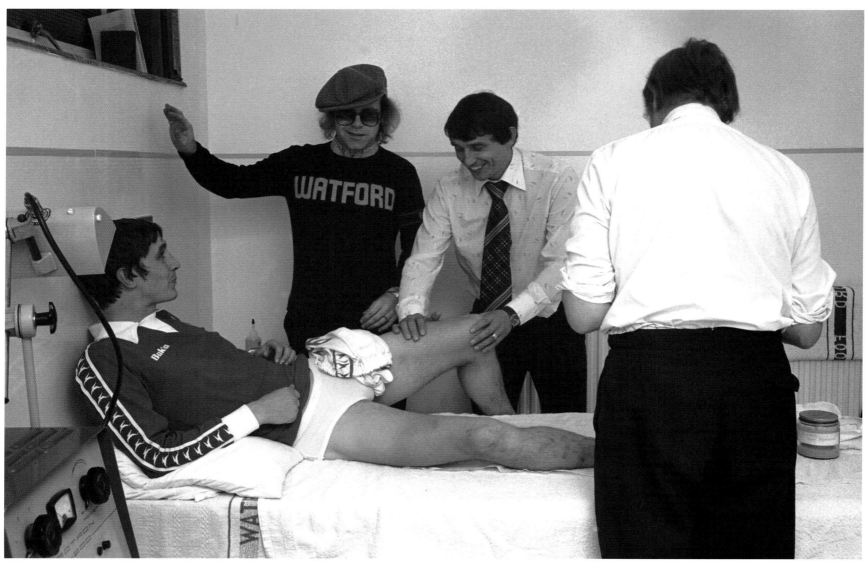

The "Chairman" created a unique bond with his team and coach that spurred the small town club to the top of English soccer...

and a red letter day in the world famous FA Cup final at Wembley which Elton had regularly filled as a performer

Elton stepped down as chairman of Watford FC in 1987 but remains, to this day the club's president with a significant financial interest

Graham Taylor, the young coach he hired to transform the club into a power in football went on to coach the England team

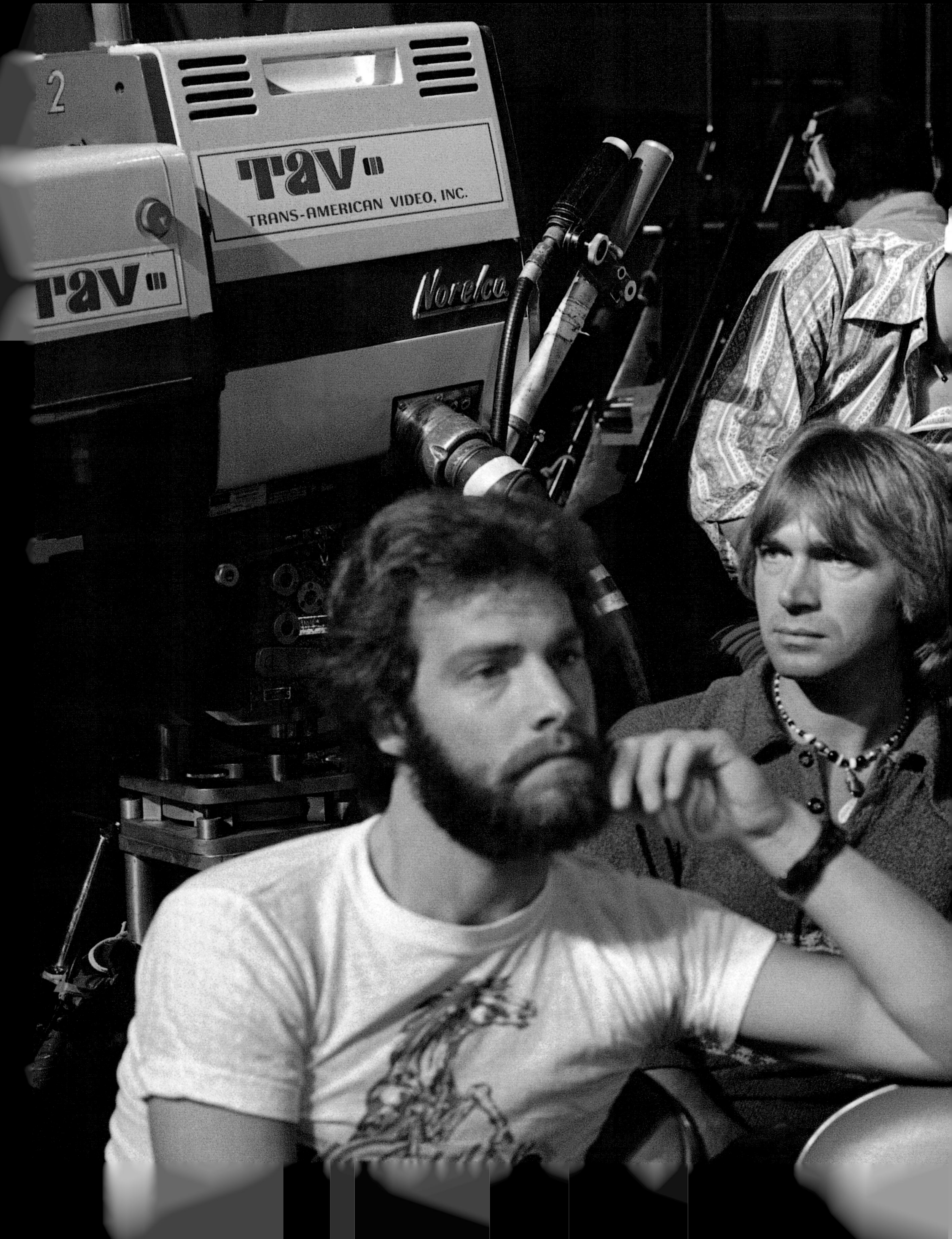
2
TAV
TRANS-AMERICAN VIDEO, INC.
TAV
Norelco

At a Los Angeles music awards ceremony in 1975, Elton and Diana Ross play up for the camera during rehearsals

Showtime: Ella Fitzgerald, Diana Ross, Cher and Elton go live to 40 million people on national television

To celebrate five years of success since he first appeared at the venue, Elton played four shows at The Troubadour club in Los Angeles

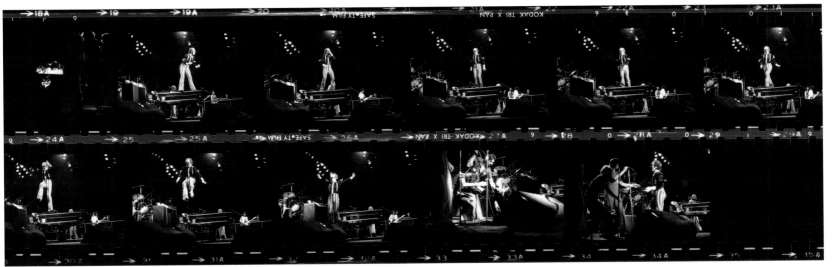

Rock of the Westies

1975 WAS PROBABLY THE HARDEST WORKING YEAR ANY MUSICIAN HAS EVER EMBARKED UPON.

INTERNATIONAL TOURS, THE CULT ROCK OPERA **TOMMY,** CONCERTS IN CLUBS AND STADIA AND TWO ALBUMS RELEASED IN THE SPACE OF SIX MONTHS – PROVIDING UNIQUE ACCESS TO THE STUDIO WORK THAT WENT INTO THEM FOR PHOTOGRAPHER **TERRY O'NEILL**

Some critics were unimpressed but *Rock Of The Westies* entered US charts at No 1 in October 1975, selling 7 million albums

No-one can quite remember how film director Michael Winner gatecrashed the sessions (above)

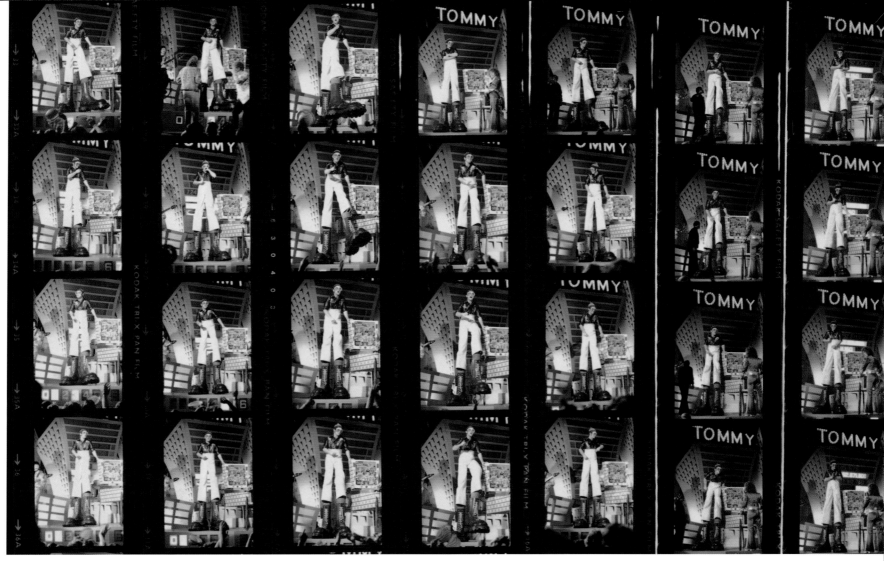

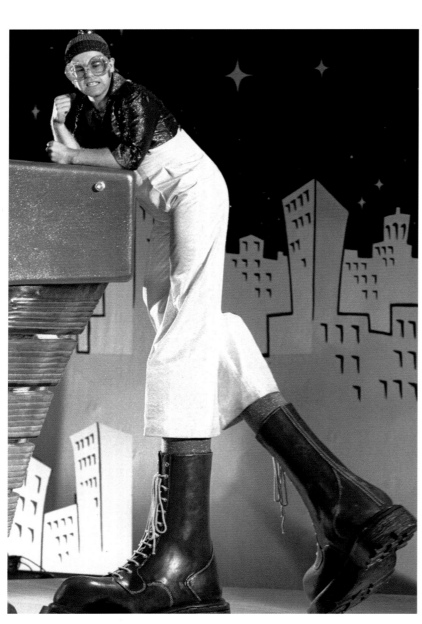

...and ended with the release of *Pinball Wizard* – Elton's signature tune from his dazzling performance with The Who's Roger Daltry in *Tommy*

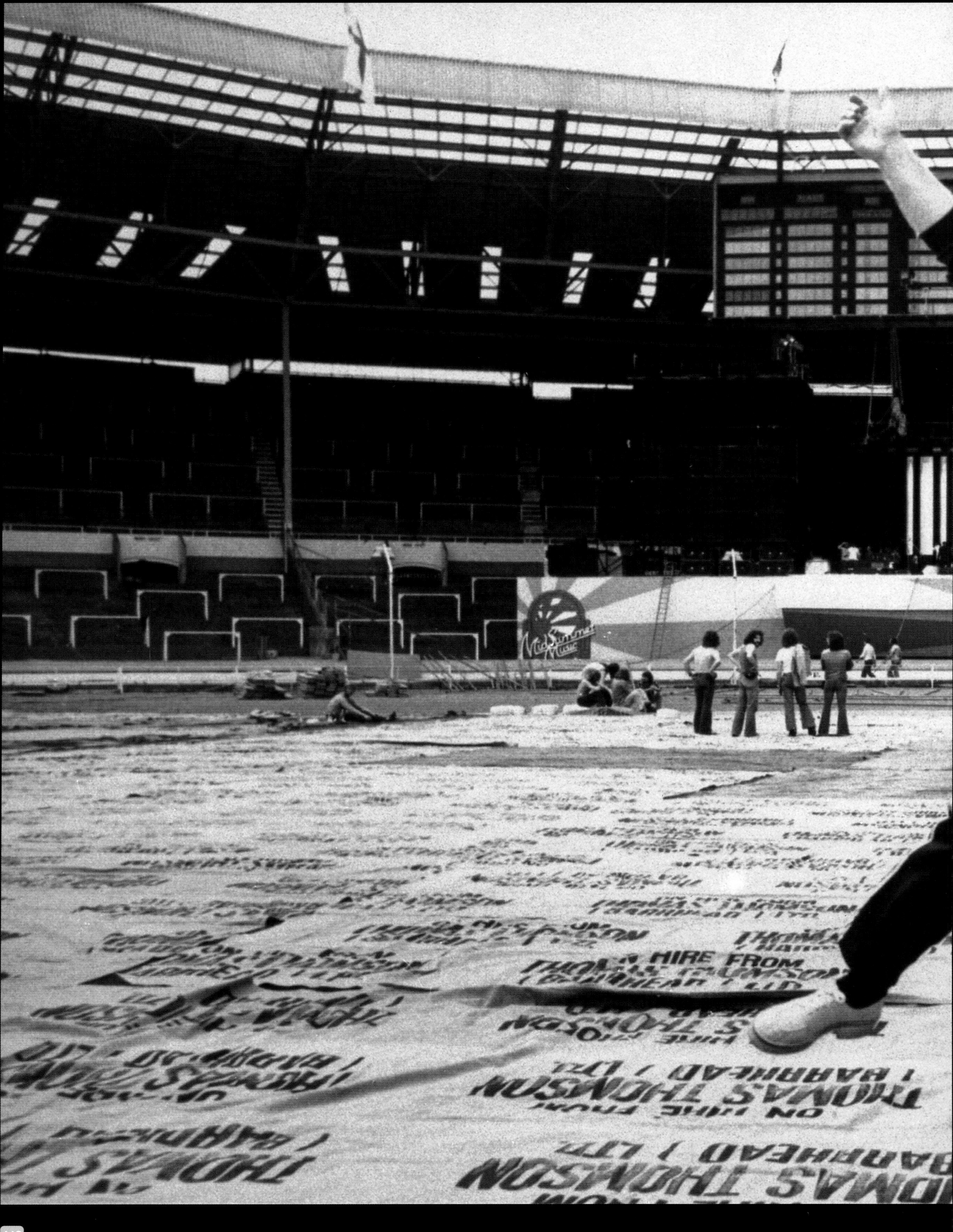
Midsummer Music
HIRE FROM

Elton in Wembley Stadium, soon to be filled-to-the-rafters with 75,000 fans 113

After five tumultuous years on the road and in the studio, the strain started to tell and Elton began taking time out...

...to see old friends including Paul and Linda McCartney, Ringo Starr, Cartier and Aspreys

Indulging his passion for tennis Elton's close friendship with the legendary Billie Jean King meant free lessons at the Queens Club in London

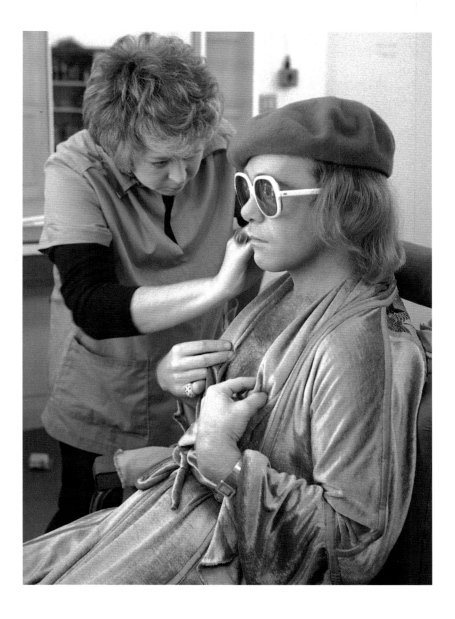

In 1977 Elton was changing his image and agreed to appear on the show if he didn't have to wear his now discarded flamboyant stage costumes. Jim Henson proved persuasive

Satin jump suits, sequin studded, monogrammed grand pianos, Elton's last concerts were a farewell to the frippery

In late 1976 Elton told *Rolling Stone* he was bisexual – it signalled the end of outrageous performances and heralded a new era as the Rocket Man sought a more sober and mature image

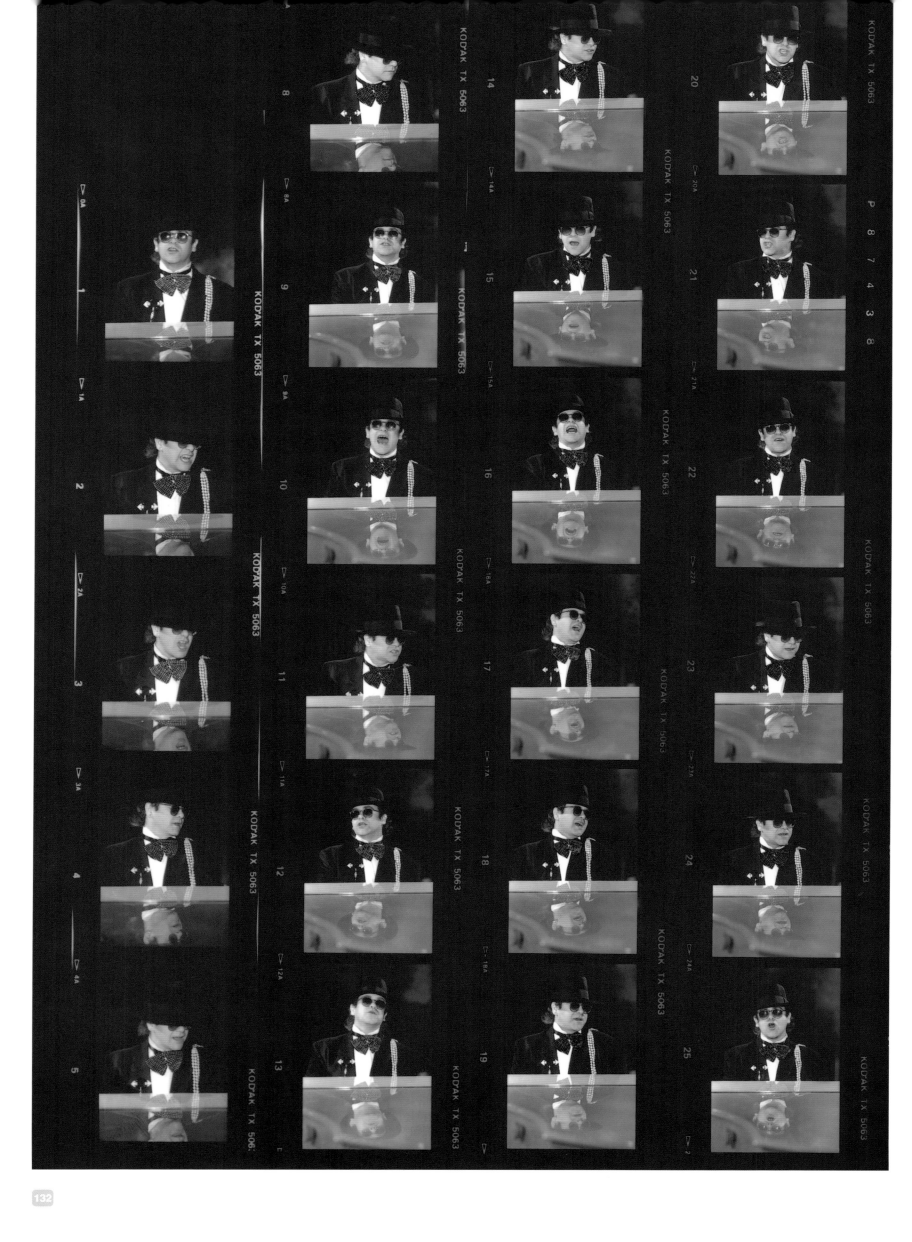

I'm Still Standing and *I Guess That's Why They Call It The Blues* were timeless classics that emerged in the 80s as Elton sought a more restful and grounded lifestyle

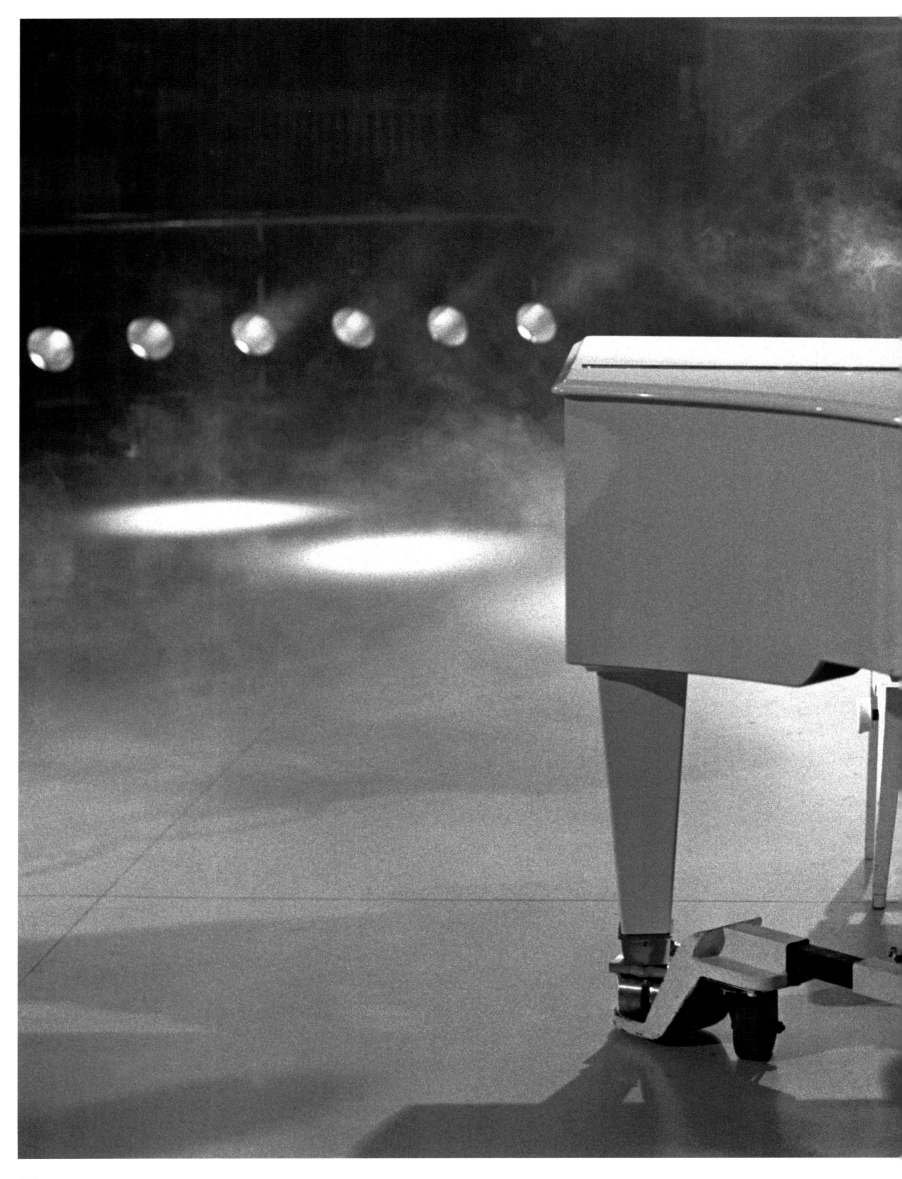

But the concerts continued, with Elton throwing himself into performing free for good causes, from HIV awareness campaigns to *Live Aid*

A 70s classic that adorns private art collections, Elton on his bed at home in Windsor, outside London

Throughout the **Elton John** roller coaster years, **Terry O'Neill** was commissioned to undertake scores of **portrait sessions**, for publicity stills, albums and magazine covers

A FAME THE SIZE OF ELTON'S REQUIRED A CONSTANT AND VARIED DIET OF IMAGES TO FEED THE FRENZIED APPETITES OF THE WORLD'S MEDIA – AND TO KEEP UP WITH THE PRODIGIOUS OUTPUT OF ONE OF THE WORLD'S GREATEST MUSICAL TALENTS, THE PHOTOGRAPHS HAD TO BE REFRESHED BY NEW IDEAS AND IMAGERY

UNLIKE ON STAGE IN FRONT OF 100,000 FANS, ELTON WAS **NEVER COMPLETELY COMFORTABLE SITTING FOR THE CAMERA** – THE SHOWMAN POSED BUT THE MAN BEHIND THE ICON REMAINED MODESTLY UNNERVED BY THE ATTENTION OF ONE ARTIST PUTTING ANOTHER **IN FOCUS**

In private at home on the exercise machine Elton could forget the camera...

but in the studio the image had to be exuberant

Another 70s "at home" classic. Elton poses in his orangery, but nobody remembers where the white rabbit came from

It's 1974 and Elton's eyewear and costumes have become his trademark

Even his spectacles were designed to match his clothes

Elton seemed to have a suit and a pair of eyeglasses for every hour of the day

**ELTON WORKED HARD
ON HIS PUBLIC FACE**
BUT BEHIND THE
GLAMOUR AND GLITZ
THERE'S A QUIET SOUL
TERRY O'NEILL

To 2755

O'Neill searched his memory to date this studio shoot but the 70s were such a blur that one shoot merged into another

153

In the sitting room at Elton's house he experimented with different portraits to find potential album covers

Inside Elton's dressing room clothes, shoes and accessories spilled over. O'Neill wondered how many had ever seen the light of day

WHAT NEXT?
AS ELTON PONDERED
HIS NEXT COSTUME
CHANGE, O'NEILL
SPOTTED THE FIRST
EVER PIN-UP PICTURE
OF MARILYN MONROE
IN A CALENDAR FROM
THE EARLY 50s AND
CLICKED THE
SHUTTER

Yes, he really is asleep. There were times when Elton couldn't keep his eyes open – but O'Neil did

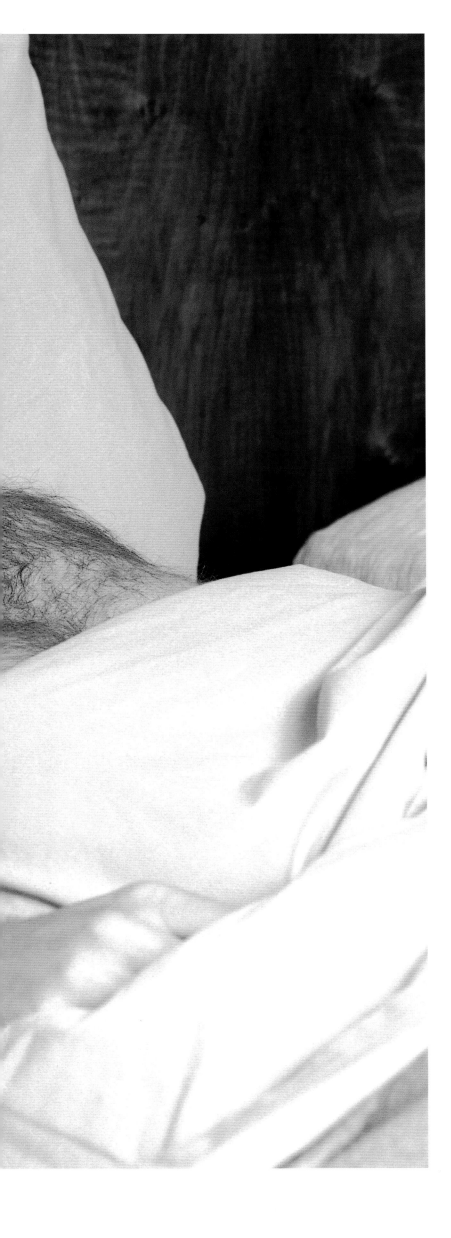

Elton with style icon, broadcaster and original presenter of the hit British TV show, *Ready Steady Go* – Cathy MGowan

Elton naps in the office of his 70s business manager John Reid

An airing for the embroidered butterfly jumpsuit

The unparalleled success of 1975 found Elton unimpressed by his waxworks inauguration at Madame Tussauds in London

The Elton John band, 1974

The portrait session for Elton's *A Single Man* album in 1978 at Windsor Castle

A Single Man's cover shot had to be perfect and O'Neill tried it from every angle in very unreliable weather conditions

Elton was an avid collector of art. Eventually he had to make a choice – sell some or buy another house (he had four already) to fill

Every picture tells a story – but which portrait to choose? O'Neill went for the happiest shot of Elton in this early 80s shoot

With Bernie Taupin outside a Paris brasserie in 1980 on a day – and a night – of shooting

Elton in Paris with Taupin and an array of costumes which he would later put up for auction

O'Neill hit on the idea of Elton wielding a firework at night in a Parisian back alley to add drama to the imagery he was collecting

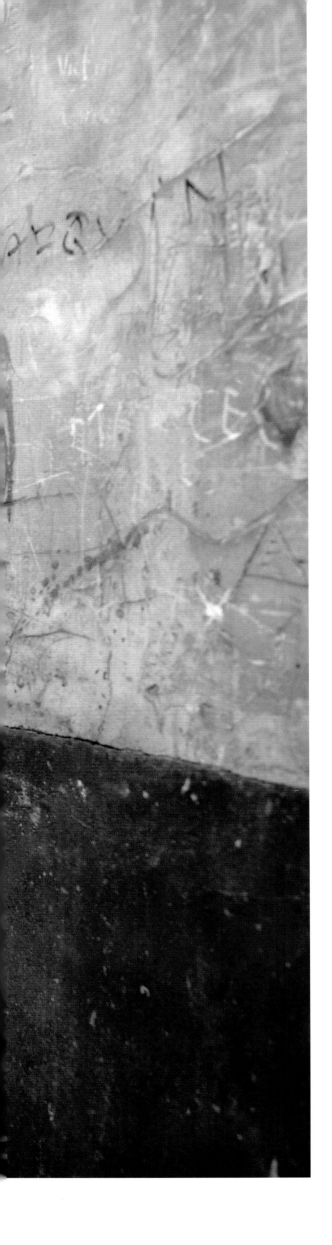

TO 110385 Y

Back home in the mid 80s, Elton is ever the dandy

194 Elton and Paul backstage before the momentous *Live Aid* concert at Wembley...

it was the world's greatest televised event in history and raised millions for starving people in Africa

The first of a portrait series to publicise the auction of Elton's personal items at Sotheby's

Costumes, art, accessories, even cars went under the hammer – and raised in excess of $20 million

Elton posed in numerous outfits to illustrate the sale catalogue which stretched to three volumes

One of many collaborations with other artists, Billy Joel and Elton embarked on their *Face To Face* tour in 1998 – one of four tours the duo have done together

Another bed, another hotel, another gig. Elton has probably performed live more than any living honoree in the Rock Hall Of Fame, over the past four decades

Backstage, believed to be Madison Square Garden in New York City in 2004. O'Neill has lost count of the dressing rooms he's photographed backstage at Elton concerts

YOU CAN'T HELP BUT LOVE ELTON

HE'S A GENIUS, AN ENIGMA, A STAR, POSSIBLY
ONE OF THE GREATEST OF ALL TIME
TERRY O'NEILL

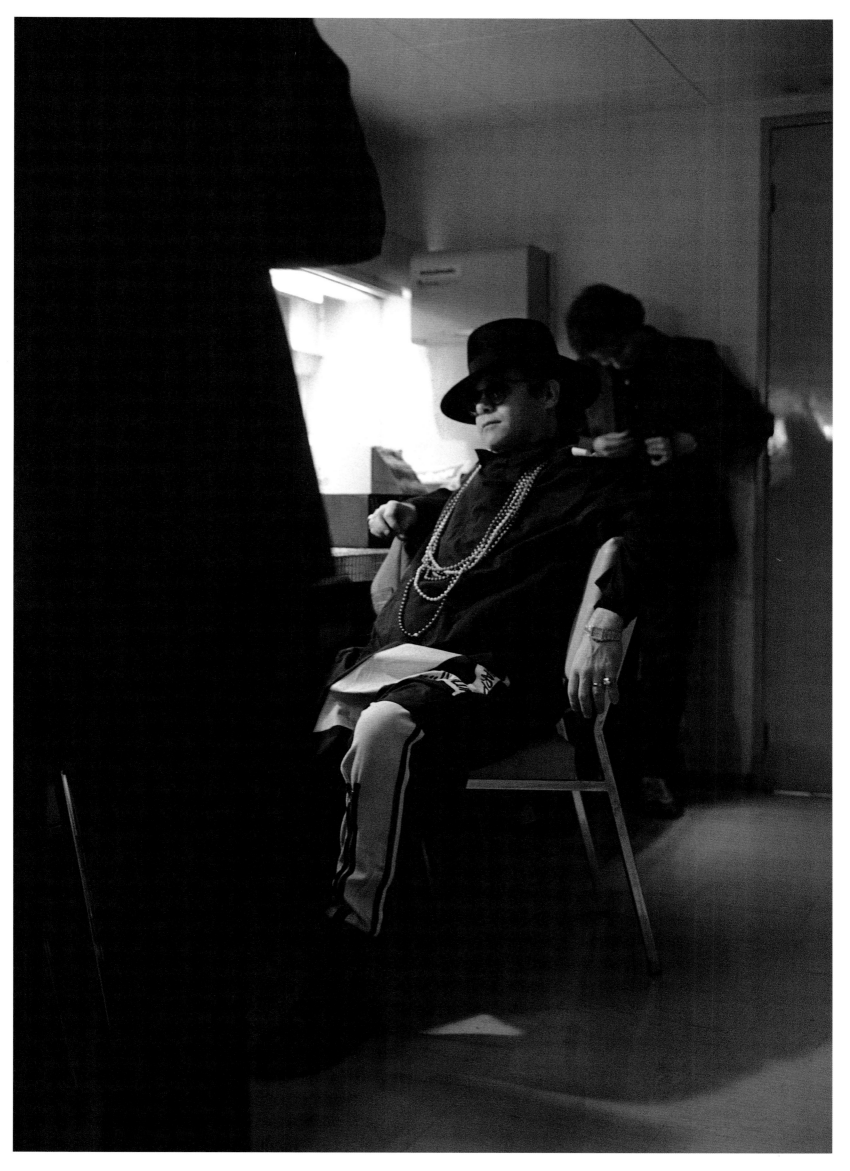

Elton John is about to enter his fifth decade in showbusiness since teaming up with Bernie Taupin in 1968 to write their first songs together

Discography

Albums

Empty Sky
Release Date: June 3, 1969 (UK),
January 13, 1975 (US)
Chart Positions: UK -, US No. 6

Elton John
Release Date: April 10, 1970 (UK),
July 22, 1970 (US)
Chart Positions: UK No. 11, US No. 4

Tumbleweed Connection
Release Date: October 30, 1970 (UK),
January 4, 1971 (US)
Chart Positions: UK No. 6, US No. 5

Madman Across the Water
Release Date: November 5, 1971 (UK),
November 15, 1971 (US)
Chart Positions: UK No. 41, US No. 8

Honky Château
Release Date: May 19, 1972 (UK),
May 26, 1972 (US)
Chart Positions: UK No. 2, US No. 1 (5)

**Don't Shoot Me I'm Only
the Piano Player**
Release Date: January 22, 1973 (UK),
January 26, 1973 (US)
Chart Positions: UK No. 1 (6),
US No. 1 (2)

Goodbye Yellow Brick Road
Release Date: October 5, 1973 (UK),
October 5, 1973 (US)
Chart Positions: UK No. 1 (2),
US No. 1 (8)

Caribou
Release Date: June 28, 1974 (UK),
June 24, 1974 (US)
Chart Positions: UK No. 1 (2),
US No. 1 (4)

**Captain Fantastic and the
Brown Dirt Cowboy**
Release Date: May 23, 1975 (UK),
May 19, 1975 (US)
Chart Positions: UK No. 2, US No. 1 (7)
Certifications: 3 x Platinum (US), 2 x
Platinum (UK)

Rock of the Westies
Release Date: October 4, 1975 (UK),
October 20, 1975 (US)
Chart Positions: UK No. 5, US No. 1 (3)

Blue Moves
Release Date: October 22, 1976 (UK),
October 28, 1976 (US)
Chart Positions: UK No. 3, US No. 3

A Single Man
Release Date: October 10, 1978 (UK),
October 1978 (US)
Chart Positions: UK No. 8, US No. 15

Victim of Love
Release Date: October 13, 1979 (UK),
October 1979 (US)
Chart Positions: UK No. 41, US No. 35
21 at 33
Release Date: May 13, 1980 (UK),
May 1980 (US)
Chart Positions: UK No. 12, US No. 13

The Fox
Release Date: May 20, 1981 (UK),
May 22, 1981 (US)
Chart Positions: UK No. 12, US No. 21

Jump Up!
Release Date: April 9, 1982 (UK),
April 1982 (US)
Chart Positions: UK No. 13, US No. 17

Too Low for Zero
Release Date: June 1983 (UK),
May 23, 1983 (US)
Chart Positions: UK No. 7, US No. 25

Breaking Hearts
Release Date: June 1984 (UK),
June 1984 (US)
Chart Positions: UK No. 2, US No. 20

Ice on Fire
Release Date: November 1985 (UK),
November 1985 (US)
Chart Positions: UK No. 3, US No. 48

Leather Jackets
Release Date: November 1986 (UK),
November 1986 (US)
Chart Positions: UK No. 24, US No. 91

Reg Strikes Back
Release Date: June 1988 (UK),
June 1988 (US)
Chart Positions: UK No. 18, US No. 16

Sleeping with the Past
Release Date: September 1989 (UK),
August 1989 (US)
Chart Positions: UK No. 1 (5),
US No. 23

The One
Release Date: June 22, 1992 (UK),
June 26, 1992 (US)
Chart Positions: UK No. 2, US No. 8

Duets
Release Date: November 1993 (UK),
November 30, 1993 (US)
Chart Positions: UK No. 5, US No. 25

Made in England
Release Date: March 20, 1995 (UK),
March 21, 1995 (US)
Chart Positions: UK No. 3, US No. 13

The Big Picture
Release Date: September 22, 1997
(UK), September 23, 1997 (US)
Chart Positions: UK No. 3, US No. 9

Songs from the West Coast
Release Date: October 1, 2001 (UK),
October 2, 2001 (US)
Chart Positions: UK No. 2, US No. 15

Peachtree Road
Release Date: November 8, 2004 (UK),
November 9, 2004 (US)
Chart Positions: UK No. 21, US No. 17

The Captain & The Kid
Release Date: September 18, 2006
(UK), September 19, 2006 (US)
Chart Positions: UK No. 6 (UK),
US No. 18

HOLLYWOOD AND BROADWAY

ELTON JOHN HAS UNDERTAKEN A SERIES
OF PROJECTS IN BOTH FILM AND MUSICALS,
APPLYING HIS MUSIC WRITING TALENT:

In 1971, he wrote the soundtrack for the movie **Friends**
In 1972 he appeared in Marc Bolan's musical film **Born to Boogie**
In 1975, he appeared as the Pinball Wizard in Ken Russell's movie version
of the rock opera **Tommy**
In 1994 with Tim Rice he wrote songs for Walt Disney's **The Lion King**
In 1998 with Tim Rice he composed the music for the Disney production
of **Aida**. They received the Tony Award for Best Original Score
and the Grammy Award for Best Musical Show Album
In 1999 John wrote the score for **The Muse**
In 2000 he composed songs for DreamWorks' animated film **The Road
to El Dorado**
In 2001, his 1970s songs **Tiny Dancer** and **Mona Lisas and
Mad Hatters** were featured on the **Almost Famous** soundtrack
In 2001, he appeared as animated character John in the popular
children's television series **Bob the Builder**, in an episode called
"A Christmas to Remember"
In 2003 his song **The Heart of Every Girl** was featured as the
end title song for **Mona Lisa Smile**
In 2005 **My Father's Gun** (from the Tumbleweed Connection album),
was featured in **Elizabethtown**
In 2005 John composed music for the UK West End production of
Billy Elliot the Musical (2005) with Lee Hall
In 2006 he composed the music for the short-lived Broadway musical
Lestat: The musical. He also released Elton **John's
Christmas Party** with two of his songs and the rest being
various artists that same year.

LIVE ALBUMS

17-11-70
1971, UK No. 20, US No. 11
Here and There
1976, UK No. 6, US No. 4
A Single Man In Moscow
1979
Elton John live in Australia with the Melbourne Symphony Orchestra
1987, UK No. 43, US No. 24
Elton John One Night Only – The Greatest Hits
2000, UK No. 7, US No. 65

SOUNDTRACKS, SCORES & THEATRE ALBUMS

Friends
1971, US No. 36
The Lion King
1994, US No. 1 (9) Certified (US) Diamond
Elton John and Tim Rice's Aida
1998, UK No. 29, US No. 41
The Muse
1999
The Road to El Dorado
2000, US No. 63
Billy Elliot The Musical
2005, [original cast recording]

COMPILATIONS

Elton John's Greatest Hits
1974, UK No. 1 (11), US No. 1 (10) (Certified (US) Diamond)
Elton John's Greatest Hits Vol. II
1977, UK No. 6, US No. 21
Lady Samantha
1980, UK No. 56
Elton John's Milestones
1980
Your Songs
1985
Elton John's Greatest Hits Vol. 3
1987, US No. 84
To Be Continued
1990, US No. 82; RIAA Certified Platinum on 28/11/06
The Very Best of Elton John
1990, UK No. 1 (2)
Rare Masters
1992
Elton John's Greatest Hits 1976-1986
1992
Chartbusters Go Pop!
1994, 20 Legendary Covers from 1969/70 as Sung by Elton John
Classic Elton John
1994
Love Songs
1996, UK No. 4, US No. 24
Greatest Hits 1970-2002
2002, UK No. 3, US No. 12
Elton John's Christmas Party
2005, (other various artists) (re-released in 2006 with less tracks)
Rocket Man: The Definitive Hits
2007, UK No. 2, US No. 9

TRIBUTE ALBUMS

Two Rooms: Celebrating the Songs of Elton John & Bernie Taupin
1991
The Timeless Classics Of Elton John
2006, Performed By Studio 99

DVDS

The Very Best of Elton John
2000, original video released 1990
Elton John Live in Barcelona
2000, original video released 1992
Love Songs
2001, original video released 1995
Classic Albums – Elton John:

Goodbye Yellow Brick Road
2001
Elton John One Night Only: The Greatest Hits Live at Madison Square Garden
2001
Live In Australia
2003, original video released 1987
To Russia with Elton
2004, original video released 1980s
Dream Ticket
2004, 4-Disc Box Set
Two Rooms: Celebrating the Songs of Elton John & Bernie Taupin
2005, original video released 1991
Elton 60 – Live at Madison Square Garden
2007, 2 DVD set

Singles

A Word In Spanish
All That I'm Allowed I'm Thankful
Believe
Bennie and the Jets
Bite Your Lip Get Up and Dance
Blessed
Blue Eyes
Border Song
Breaking Hearts Ain't What It Used to Be
Can You Feel the Love Tonight?
Candle In the Wind
Candle in the Wind
Circle of Life
Club At the End Of the Street
Cold As Christmas
Crazy Water
Crocodile Rock
Cry To heaven
Daniel
Don't Go Breaking My Heart
Don't Let The Sun Go Down On Me
Don't Let The Sun Go Down On Me
Easier To Walk Away
Ego (bonus track)
Empty Gardens Hey Hey johnny
Flinstone Boy (bonus track)
Friends
Goodbye Yellow Brick Road
Grow Some Funk Of Your Own
Healing Hands
Heartache All Over the World
Honky cat
I Don't Wanna Go On With You Like That
I Guess That's Why They Call It the Blues
I Saw Her Standing There
I Want Love
I've Been Loving You
If the River Can Bend
In Neon
Island Girl
It's Me That You Need
Johnny B. Goode
Kiss the Bride
Lady Samantha
Levon
Little Jeannie
Lucy In the Sky with Diamonds
Made In England

Nikita
Nobody Wins
Original Sin
Part Time Love
Passengers
Philadelphia Freedom
Pinball Wizard
Please
Recover Your Soul
Rock n Roll Madonna
Rocket man/ I Think It's Going to Be a Long Long Time
Runaway Train
Sacrifice
Sad Songs Say So Much
Satorial Eloquence
Saturday Night's Alright For Fighting
Simple Life
Slow Rivers
Someday Out Of the Blue (Theme from El Dorado)
Someone Saved My Life Tonight
Something About the Way You Look Tonight
Song For Guy
Sorry Seems To Be the Hardest Word
Sorry Seems to be the Hardest Word
Step Into Christmas
The Bitch Is Back
The Bridge
The Last Song
The One
This Train Don't Stop There Anymore
Tinderbox
Tiny Dancer
Town Of Plenty
True Love
Turn the Lights Out When You Leave
Victim Of Love
Who Wears These Shoes
Wrap Her up
Written In the Stars
Your Song
Your Song (with Alessandro Safina)

TO 2758